P9-DHS-488

D0015189

SOUTH AMERICA
TODAY

CHILE

PERU

BOLIVIA

BRAZIL

PARAGUAY

Iquique

Antofagasta

Atacama Desert

Llullaillaco
Volcano

ANDES MOUNTAINS

PARAGUAY

URUGUAY

Juan Fernández
Islands

Viña del Mar
Valparaíso

Santiago

C H I L E

ARGENTINA

ATLANTIC
OCEAN

Talcahuano
Concepción

Temuco

Valdivia

Puerto Montt

Chiloé
Island

Los Chonos
Archipelago

ANDES MOUNTAINS

PACIFIC

OCEAN

Wellington
Island

N

W   E

S

Punta Arenas

Santa Inés
Island

Strait of
Magellan

Tierra del Fuego

Cape Horn

0   250   500 Miles

0   250   500 Kilometers

Sinusoidal Projection

20°S

30°S

40°S

50°S

90°W   80°W   70°W   60°W   50°W   40°W

SOUTH AMERICA TODAY

CHILE

Charles J. Shields

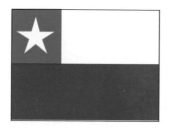

Mason Crest Publishers
Philadelphia

Produced by OTTN Publishing, Stockton, N.J.

Mason Crest Publishers
370 Reed Road
Broomall, PA 19008
www.masoncrest.com

First printing

1 3 5 7 9 8 6 4 2

Library of Congress Cataloging-in-Publication Data

  Shields, Charles J., 1951-
    Chile / Charles J. Shields.
        p. cm. — (South America today)
    Includes index.
    ISBN 978-1-4222-0634-8 (hardcover) — ISBN 978-1-4222-0701-7 (pbk.)
  1. Chile—Juvenile literature. [1. Chile] I. Title.
    F3058.5.S55 2008
    983—dc22
                                          2008032311

SOUTH AMERICA
TODAY

Argentina		Paraguay
Bolivia	South America:	Peru
Brazil	Facts & Figures	Suriname
Chile	Ecuador	Uruguay
Colombia	Guyana	Venezuela

Table of Contents

Introduction   6
James D. Henderson

Land of the Andes   9

Slow March to Democracy   19

A Robust Economy   29

Chile's People and Culture   37

Old Cities with Fresh Outlooks   43

A Calendar of Chilean Festivals   50

Recipes   52

Glossary   54

Project and Report Ideas   56

Chronology   58

Further Reading/Internet Resources   60

For More Information   61

Index   62

Discovering South America

James D. Henderson

South America is a cornucopia of natural resources, a treasure house of ecological variety. It is also a continent of striking human diversity and geographic extremes. Yet in spite of that, most South Americans share a set of cultural similarities. Most of the continent's inhabitants are properly termed "Latin" Americans. This means that they speak a Romance language (one closely related to Latin), particularly Spanish or Portuguese. It means, too, that most practice Roman Catholicism and share the Mediterranean cultural patterns brought by the Spanish and Portuguese who settled the continent over five centuries ago.

Still, it is never hard to spot departures from these cultural norms. Bolivia, Peru, and Ecuador, for example, have significant Indian populations who speak their own languages and follow their own customs. In Paraguay the main Indian language, Guaraní, is accepted as official along with Spanish. Nor are all South Americans Catholics. Today Protestantism is making steady gains, while in Brazil many citizens practice African religions right along with Catholicism and Protestantism.

South America is a lightly populated continent, having just 6 percent of the world's people. It is also the world's most tropical continent, for a larger percentage of its land falls between the tropics of Cancer and Capricorn than is the case with any other continent. The world's driest desert is there, the Atacama in northern Chile, where no one has ever seen a drop of rain fall. And the world's wettest place is there too, the Chocó region of Colombia, along that country's border with Panama. There it rains almost every day. South America also has some of the world's highest mountains, the Andes,

Laguna Miscanti is a high-altitude tourist attraction in Chile.

and its greatest river, the Amazon.

So welcome to South America! Through this colorfully illustrated series of books you will travel through 12 countries, from giant Brazil to small Suriname. On your way you will learn about the geography, the history, the economy, and the people of each one. Geared to the needs of teachers and students, each volume contains book and web sources for further study, a chronology, project and report ideas, and even recipes of tasty and easy-to-prepare dishes popular in the countries studied. Each volume describes the country's national holidays and the cities and towns where they are held. And each book is indexed.

You are embarking on a voyage of discovery that will take you to lands not so far away, but as interesting and exotic as any in the world.

A wide variety of climates and geographic features can be found within Chile. (Opposite) Snow-capped Mount Osorno, a volcano in the Andes, rises more than 8,500 feet (2,593 meters) over Lake Llanquihue in Patagonia. (Right) The Atacama Desert is the driest spot on earth, averaging just .002 inches (.005 cm) of rain a year.

1 Land of the Andes

CHILE IS A country of extreme beauty and startling contrasts. Attractions range from the towering volcanic peaks of the Andes to the foggy ancient forests of the Lake District. On the other hand, the Atacama Desert, one of the world's driest regions, is also one of the most inhospitable places on earth.

Chile stretches through more than 38 degrees of latitude: the tropic of Capricorn cuts through the north of the country, while at its southernmost extreme Chile lies closer to the Antarctic Circle than any other country. This great north-south extension has given Chile a range of climates.

A Ribbon-Like Country

From north to south, Chile—located in southwestern South America—runs about 2,650 miles (4,265 kilometers), roughly the distance between

The stone statues of Easter Island (called *moai*) have fascinated visitors for hundreds of years. On average the nearly 900 *moai* stand 13 feet (4 meters) high and weigh 14 tons, though the largest erected statue is nearly 33 feet

San Francisco and New York. But its average width is less than 110 miles (177 km), and this ribbon-like country is more than 18 times longer than its widest point. Chile's total area of 292,135 square miles (756,338 square kilometers) makes it about twice the size of Montana. The country has 3,999 miles (6,435 km) of coastline.

(9.8 meters) high and weighs 82 tons. The *moai* were carved from volcanic rock between A.D. 1400 and 1600 by the indigenous people of Easter Island, Polynesians who called themselves Rapa Nui.

Chile is bounded on the north by Peru, on the east by Bolivia and Argentina, and on the south and west by the Pacific Ocean. *Archipelagoes* extend along the southern Chilean coast from Chiloé Island to Cape Horn, the southernmost point of the South American continent. Among these are the Chonos Archipelago, Wellington Island, and the western portion of Tierra del Fuego. Other islands belonging to Chile include the Juan Fernández Islands, Easter Island, and Sala y Gómez, all of which lie in the South Pacific. At the southernmost tip of Chile are sea-lanes between the Atlantic and Pacific Oceans—the Strait of Magellan, Beagle Channel, and Drake Passage.

The most outstanding physical feature of slender Chile is the massive, almost impassable wall of the Andes Mountains, which extend the entire length of the country from the Bolivian plateau in the north to Tierra del Fuego in the south. The Andes mountain range, which contains more than 50 active volcanic peaks, is still rising. Chile lies in a zone of geologic instability—in addition to volcanic activity, it is subject to severe earthquakes.

Chile's mineral resources are limited in number, but the deposits are large and rich. Natural resources include nitrates, iron ore, coal, molybdenum, manganese, petroleum and natural gas, silver, and gold.

Three Topographic Zones

Chile can be divided length-ways into three major *topographic* zones. The towering Andean *cordillera* is located to the east. To the west are low coastal mountains overlooking a narrow strip of lower land along the Pacific Ocean. In between the mountain ranges is the third topographic zone—the plateau area, which includes the fertile Central Valley.

The Andes are widest in Chile's northern region, forming broad plateaus and containing many mountains with elevations higher than 20,000 feet (6,100 m). The country's highest peaks, Cerro Aconcagua (22,834 feet, or 6,960 m) and Ojos del Salado (22,572 feet, or 6,885 meters), can be found on the border with Argentina. In the north, the plateau area is occupied by the great Atacama Desert, which contains vast nitrate fields and rich mineral deposits.

In the center of the country is the river-fed Central Valley, 600 miles (968 km) long, and 25 to 50 miles (40 to 81 km) wide. Major mountain passes cut through the Andes here, giving access to the country's finest natural harbors. The fertile area between the Aconcagua and Bío-Bío Rivers forms the agricultural heartland of Chile. In the northern part of the Central Valley are vineyards and giant farms; in the south are primeval forests and deep, cold lakes.

In southern Chile, the land falls away. The region between mountains

Jagged peaks in scenic Torres del Paine National Park.

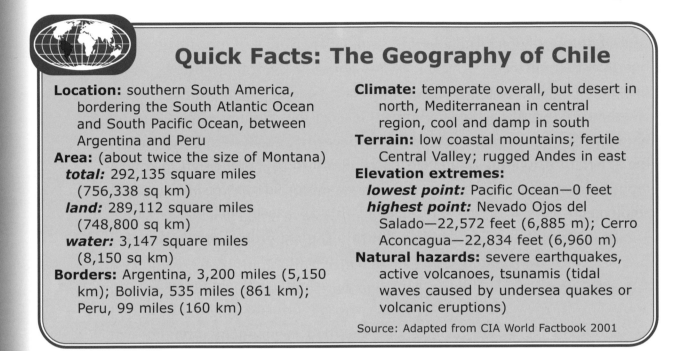

Quick Facts: The Geography of Chile

Location: southern South America, bordering the South Atlantic Ocean and South Pacific Ocean, between Argentina and Peru

Area: (about twice the size of Montana)
total: 292,135 square miles (756,338 sq km)
land: 289,112 square miles (748,800 sq km)
water: 3,147 square miles (8,150 sq km)

Borders: Argentina, 3,200 miles (5,150 km); Bolivia, 535 miles (861 km); Peru, 99 miles (160 km)

Climate: temperate overall, but desert in north, Mediterranean in central region, cool and damp in south

Terrain: low coastal mountains; fertile Central Valley; rugged Andes in east

Elevation extremes:
lowest point: Pacific Ocean—0 feet
highest point: Nevado Ojos del Salado—22,572 feet (6,885 m); Cerro Aconcagua—22,834 feet (6,960 m)

Natural hazards: severe earthquakes, active volcanoes, tsunamis (tidal waves caused by undersea quakes or volcanic eruptions)

Source: Adapted from CIA World Factbook 2001

and ocean shatters into the baffling maze of channels and islands that ends in Chilean Patagonia. Southernmost Chile is marked by Cape Horn, a treacherous *headland* surrounded by storm-tossed seas. The Strait of Magellan is the most famous route around the tip of the continent.

Many of Chile's major lakes, including Lake Llanquihue, are concentrated in the scenic Lake District of the southern region. The southern Lake District is the home of Chile's most prominent *indigenous* peoples, the Araucanians.

Chile has many rivers, but they are short. They start in the Andes and flow west to the Pacific. In the northern and central regions, the Andes, snow-topped year-round, continually feed the rivers with fresh water. The most important rivers (from north to south) are the Loa, Elqui, Aconcagua, Maipo, Maule, Bío-Bío, and Imperial. These rivers have *cascades*, limiting their usefulness for shipping and travel. However, the rivers are vital for irrigation and for providing hydroelectric power.

The far southern region is without an interior valley. The land plunges into the sea at Puerto Montt. The long chains of islands along the coast, which is indented by numerous *fjords*, are actually the peaks of the submerged coastal mountains. The southern Andes have elevations that seldom exceed 6,000 feet (1,830 meters).

Diverse Climate

Because it stretches so far from north to south, Chile has a varied climate that can be divided into three major *climatological* regions: the northern (arid), central (Mediterranean), and southern (*temperate* marine) regions. On the whole, however, the country enjoys comfortable, temperate conditions. In general, temperatures are kept moderate by the influence of the Pacific Ocean.

The northern region, for example, is almost entirely desert and is one of the driest areas in the world. But the cold Peru Current (also called the Humboldt Current) offshore keeps temperatures rather cool. The average temperature range is from 64°F to 74°F (18°C to 23°C) in January and from 53°F to 62°F (11°C to 17°C) in July. (Because Chile is in the Southern Hemisphere, its seasons are opposite from those of North America.) In Chile's largest city, Santiago—located in the center of the country—the average temperature range is 54°F to 85°F (12°C to 30° C) in January and 38°F to 58°F (3°C to 14°C) in July. Temperatures decrease about 1 degree Fahrenheit for each 275 feet (84 meters) of elevation in the Andes.

Rainfall increases southward, and the central region experiences a Mediterranean-like climate. Precipitation here occurs mainly during the winter months (May to August) and ranges from an average annual total of 14 inches (35.6 centimeters) at Santiago to 0.1 inch (.254 cm) at Antofagasta. Winters are mild, and summers are relatively cool.

Magellanic penguins cluster on Magdalena Island in the Strait of Magellan. The most common species of penguin, these birds grow to about 2 feet tall. They are named for the explorer Ferdinand Magellan, whose crew hunted them for food during Magellan's 16th-century voyage around the world.

The far southern region is even cooler and experiences year-round rainfall. Precipitation reaches a maximum of about 200 inches (508 cm) near the Strait of Magellan, much of it in the form of snow. The average annual temperature at Punta Arenas in the far south is about 44°F (7°C). Strong winds and cyclonic storms are common in the southern region.

Plants and Animals

Chile's plant life varies according to climatic zone. Parts of the Atacama Desert support virtually no life at all. Elsewhere in the dry northern region, a few varieties of vegetation, such as brambles and cacti, manage to survive. In the more humid Central Valley flourish several species of cacti, *espino* (a spiky shrub), grasses, and the Chilean pine, which produces edible nuts. Farther south are dense rain forests containing laurel, magnolia, false beech, and various species of conifers. In the extreme south are windswept, low-growing grasslands.

The Andes Mountains form a barrier that prevents animals from migrating. Chile is home to few species of animals. Indigenous mammals include the llama, alpaca, vicuña, guanaco, puma, Andean wolf, *huemal* (a large deer), *pudu* (a small deer), and chinchilla. Bird life is varied, but most of the larger South American types are not found here. Aside from several varieties of trout, which were introduced from North America, few freshwater fish live in Chilean streams and lakes. But the coastal waters of Chile are filled with fish and marine animals.

(Opposite) General Augusto Pinochet had thousands of dissidents and political opponents killed or arrested during his dictatorship, which lasted from 1973 to 1990. (Right) Mapuche Indians gathered in Santiago in August 1999 for the signing of an agreement that would direct $280 million toward the development of indigenous communities in the south of Chile.

2 Slow March to Democracy

ABOUT 10,000 YEARS ago, migrating Indians settled in fertile valleys and along the coast of what is now Chile. But the rich Central Valley of the interior—surrounded on three sides by mountains—remained largely unknown to the outside world until the middle of the 15th century.

It was then that the Incas, crossing the vast salt basins of the Atacama Desert from the north, stumbled upon the valley. Originally from the area around Cuzco in what is today Peru, the Incas conquered much of the Andes region, establishing a mighty empire. But upon entering the Central Valley the Incas encountered the Mapuche, one of the three Araucanian tribes who occupied the region. The warlike Mapuche offered stiff resistance, eventually halting the Incas' advance at the Río Maule, about halfway down the 500-mile-long valley.

By 1533 the Spanish, led by Francisco Pizarro, had conquered Peru and claimed the Inca Empire's unbelievable stores of gold and silver. Two years later one of Pizarro's associates, the *conquistador* Diego de Almagro, set off from Peru in search of similar riches to the south. Almagro and his 600 soldiers, the first Europeans to enter what is today Chile, suffered incredible hardships. Though they encountered a multitude of Indians, including the fierce Araucanians, the conquistadors didn't find the hoards of gold and silver they were seeking. Yet some of them did recognize the potential of the Central Valley as a rich farmland.

After returning to Peru in 1537, Almagro became embroiled in a war with other conquistadors and was killed. Another of Pizarro's commanders, Pedro de Valdivia, set off to conquer Chile in 1540. Valdivia founded Santiago in 1541 and a handful of other Spanish settlements in the years that followed, but the Araucanians proved extremely difficult to subdue. By the early 1550s Valdivia had pushed south to the Bío-Bío River and beyond, founding Concepción and the city that still bears his name. In 1553, however, Valdivia lost his life in an Araucanian attack.

By the end of the 16th century, the Araucanians had forced the Spanish north of the Bío-Bío River, maintaining control of the southern region of Chile until the late 1880s. Elsewhere periodic, often brutal conflicts between the Indians and the Spanish continued throughout the colonial period.

In Chile, unlike other Spanish possessions in the hemisphere, Catholic missionaries had little success converting the indigenous peoples, and comparatively few Indians could be forced to work for the Spanish. Also, for various reasons, large numbers of black African slaves were never imported into Chile. This led to a social situation that was somewhat unusual in the Spanish empire. *Mestizos,* people of mixed white and Indian ancestry, became Chile's underclass. They toiled in mines or as landless peasants on the huge agricultural estates owned by the very small white minority. These estates, many located in the Central Valley, grew steadily during the 17th and 18th centuries.

Despite their wealth and privileged position in society, simmering resentments emerged among Chile's *criollos*— the whites of pure Spanish ancestry who had been born in the Western Hemisphere. Spain collected taxes from them and appointed their governors, usually reserving the most important posts for *peninsulares* (Spaniards born in Spain). Many criollos grumbled that the situation was unfair.

Independence from Spain

During the first decades of the 19th century, events in Europe would set in

This Mochica sculpture of a warrior, created around A.D. 300, is preserved in a museum in Santiago, Chile. The Mochica were an ancient people who flourished in northwestern South America from around 200 B.C. to A.D. 800.

motion the process that eventually led to Chile's independence from Spain. In 1808 Napoleon Bonaparte, the emperor of France, *deposed* Spain's king, Ferdinand VII, and placed his brother Joseph Bonaparte on the Spanish throne. In Chile, a national *junta* composed of *criollos* and professing loyalty to Ferdinand took control of the colony on September 18, 1810. Their real agenda, however, was complete independence for Chile.

Soon, though, two powerful military leaders emerged in Chile. Though both favored independence, they differed in their other goals. The first, José Miguel Carrera, seemed bent on completely remaking Chilean society. The second, Bernardo O'Higgins, was somewhat less radical and, therefore, more acceptable to the wealthy criollos, who wanted independence from Spain but did not want to give up their privileged position in society. The armies of the two men appeared to be headed for a showdown. But in 1814, Ferdinand was restored to the Spanish throne, and royalist forces captured Carrera and smashed O'Higgins's army south of Santiago, at the Battle of Rancagua. O'Higgins and his surviving soldiers fled into Argentina.

In Argentina, O'Higgins joined forces with José de San Martín, a hero of Argentine independence. In 1817, the armies of the two leaders crossed the Andes into Chile and decisively defeated the Spanish forces at the Battle of Chacabuco on February 12. O'Higgins was made supreme director of Chile, and exactly one year after the victory at Chacabuco, he proclaimed the country's complete independence from Spain.

The political revolt failed to bring deep social changes, though. In fact, O'Higgins's attempts to institute reforms in Chile led to his overthrow in 1823. Chilean society continued to be marked by huge inequalities, with wealth, privilege, and political power concentrated in the hands of a few landowners.

Toward the end of the 19th century, Chile's government took a series of steps to increase its authority. The first was a campaign in the south to suppress the fierce Mapuche Indians. Then, in 1881, the government signed a treaty with Argentina confirming Chilean sovereignty over the Strait of Magellan, the primary sea-lane connecting the Atlantic and Pacific Oceans. Finally, by defeating Peru and Bolivia in the War of the Pacific (1879–83), Chile expanded its territory northward by almost one-third. Valuable nitrate deposits fell into Chilean hands, bringing an era of national *affluence*.

An Uneven Political Climate

Chile established a parliamentary-style democracy in the late 19th century. But the government's aim was largely to protect the interests of the ruling *oligarchy*. A brief but bloody civil war erupted in 1890 between landowners and the growing middle class, aided by low-wage workers. During the first half of the 20th century, the governments varied from harsh to reform-minded. But no administration could develop its policies for very long.

Finally, in 1964, Christian Democrat Eduardo Frei-Montalva won the presidency and launched a period of major reform. Under the slogan "Revolution in Liberty," the Frei administration embarked on far-reaching programs designed to improve education, housing, and the rights of agricultural laborers. By 1967, however, Frei met with increasing opposition. Leftists in favor of radical social change charged that his reforms didn't go far enough. Conservatives felt their privileges threatened.

Allende and Pinochet

In 1970, by a slim margin of 36,000 ballots, voters elected Dr. Salvador Allende, an intellectual and *Socialist* who believed that workers should control the production of goods and services. Allende's "Popular Unity" party, which included Communists, called for sweeping reforms. His program included seizing commercial industries, banks, privately owned

During three years as Chile's president, the democratically elected Salvador Allende (1908–1973), a Socialist, tried to implement economic and social reforms. His policies eventually led to Chilean resistance to his administration and a U.S.-supported coup that toppled him from power in 1973.

land, and U.S.-owned copper mines and putting them under government control. *Domestic* production dropped dramatically, creating severe shortages of consumer goods, food, and manufactured products in Chile. *Inflation* reached 1,000 percent. Mass demonstrations, labor strikes, and violence by government supporters and opponents alike broke out. By 1973, Chilean society had split into two hostile camps.

On September 11, 1973, the military stormed the presidential palace. More than 3,000 people were killed in the fighting, making it the bloodiest coup in South American history. Fighter jets bombed the presidential palace while the democratically elected president was still inside. Allende reportedly committed suicide, though his supporters insisted he was murdered.

A military government, led by General Augusto Pinochet, took control of the country. Pinochet promised a complete reversal of Allende's policies. He wasted no time. The military government dissolved Congress, suspended Chile's constitution, and outlawed opposition parties. The police enforced nighttime curfews and strict limits on the media. Nationalized companies were returned to their original owners, trade barriers were cut to encourage foreign imports, and there was renewed emphasis on exports and private investment. Pinochet said his goal was to transform Chileans from workers into entrepreneurs.

Chilean society had been split by Allende's Socialist rule, and it remained divided under the new right-wing leader. But with Pinochet in charge, *dissidents* spoke out at their peril. The general maintained his iron rule with brutally repressive tactics. Thousands of people were tortured and killed, and thousands more fled into exile.

After Pinochet

A new constitution was approved by a *plebiscite* on September 11, 1980, and General Pinochet became President of the Republic for an eight-year term. In its later years, the regime gradually permitted greater freedom of assembly, speech, and association, to include trade union activity. Pinochet's supporters argued that the flourishing economy was proof of the effectiveness of his military-backed regime, but human rights violations were still widespread.

When in 1990 Pinochet stepped down, it was owing to his own miscalculation. He had gambled his one-man rule on a 1988 plebiscite and lost. But he ensured that the military remained outside the control of government. Even today, human rights groups seeking justice for the crimes committed by Pinochet and his regime often face a wall of official non-cooperation. Pinochet himself was arrested in London in 1999 at the request of a Spanish judge investigating human rights violations. But he was judged too ill to stand trial. This decision was later overturned, but he died in 2006 without being convicted of any crimes.

In the 1988 plebiscite, Chileans voted for elections to choose a new president and the majority of members of a two-chamber congress. On December 14, 1989, Christian Democrat Patricio Aylwin, the candidate of a coalition of 17 political parties, received an absolute majority of votes. President Aylwin served from 1990 to 1994. In December 1993, Christian Democrat Eduardo Frei Ruiz-Tagle (the son of former president Eduardo Frei-Montalva), replaced Aylwin as president. He would serve a six-year

Michelle Bachelet and her parents were imprisoned and tortured during the Pinochet dictatorship. As president, she pledged to make social justice an important priority in order to continue the country's healing process.

term, instead of four years, as a result of a change to the constitution in 1997. The presidential election held on December 12, 1999, failed to produce a majority for any of the six candidates, which led to an unprecedented runoff election on January 16, 2000. Ricardo Lagos Escobar of the Socialist Party and the Party for Democracy won a narrow victory, with 51.32 percent of the votes. During his six-year presidency, Lagos earned consistently high approval ratings. In 2006, Michelle Bachelet, also a member of the Socialist Party, became Chile's first woman president following a runoff. After four open, fair presidential elections, democracy in Chile seems solid.

(Opposite) A sheep farmer tends his herd. Large numbers of sheep are raised in the Tierra del Fuego and Magallanes regions of Chile. (Right) Pack horses carry their loads along a narrow trail in Patagonia.

3 A Robust Economy

SINCE WORLD WAR I (1914–18) Chile has developed industries that process the country's raw materials and manufacture consumer goods. The major products of Chile's industries are copper and other minerals, processed food, fish meal, wood and wood products, transportation equipment, cement, textiles, iron and steel, paper, and chemicals. Chile exports minerals, wood products, fish and fish meal, chemicals, fruits, and wine. Its chief trading partners are the European Union nations, the United States, Japan, and Brazil.

Copper Is King

Since the early 20th century, the Chilean economy has been dominated by the production of copper. Copper is the nation's most valuable resource, and

Chile is the world's largest producer of the mineral. Iron ore is the country's other leading mineral product. Chile also has large deposits of nitrates, iodine, sulfur, and coal, as well as silver, gold, manganese, and molybdenum (used in strengthening and hardening steel).

Since Salvador Allende's Socialist administration was overthrown in 1973, the government has played a less important role in the economy. Beginning with the Pinochet regime, most nationalized companies have been returned to private ownership.

By the 1990s Chile's economy was one of the strongest in South America, earning the country invitations to join the Asia-Pacific Economic Cooperation (APEC) forum and the North American Free Trade Agreement (NAFTA). Chile also became an associate member of MERCOSUR, or the Southern Cone Common Market, which also includes Argentina, Brazil, Paraguay, and Uruguay. Despite its economic strengths, however, Chile's unemployment rate remains stubbornly high.

Agricultural Shortfall

Although Chile has become an industrial power, producing an adequate food supply remains one of the nation's major economic problems. Agriculture is the main occupation of only about 15 percent of the population, and domestic farming produces less than half of Chile's food needs. Only about 3 percent of Chile's land is farmed.

The chief crops are wheat, potatoes, corn, beans, sugar beets, and fruit. A variety of vegetables, fruits, and grains are grown in the Central Valley, the country's primary agricultural area. The vineyards of the valley are the basis of Chile's growing wine industry. Livestock production includes beef and poultry. Sheep are raised in large numbers in the Tierra del Fuego and the Magallanes regions of Chilean Patagonia, providing wool and meat for domestic use and for export.

Chile is the Southern Hemisphere's largest exporter of fruits. Much of its crop is sent to North America, where the fresh produce enjoys a market advantage because Chile's growing season coincides with winter in North America.

The little village of Pomaire, near Santiago, is famous for its handmade pottery.

Chile has one of the largest fishing industries in South America. Principal species include mackerel, anchovy, sardine, and herring. Processing plants pack much of the fish catch for distribution.

Forests cover about one-fifth of Chile. Harvesting the forests yields both hardwoods (such as laurel) and softwoods (such as pine). Lumber, pulp, and paper are made from the annual timber cut.

A proud fisherman in Pichilemu displays his catch. Chilean sea bass has become a popular dish in American seafood restaurants.

Quick Facts: The Economy of Chile

Gross domestic product (GDP*):
$231.1 billion (purchasing power parity)
GDP per capita: $13,900
Inflation: 4.4%
Natural resources: copper, timber, iron ore, nitrates, precious metals, molybdenum, hydropower
Agriculture: (4.8% of GDP): grapes, apples, pears, onions, wheat, corn, oats, peaches, garlic, asparagus, beans; beef, poultry, wool; fish; timber (2003 est.)
Services: (63% of GDP): tourism, banking, government services (2003 est)
Industry: (23.4% of GDP): copper, other minerals, foodstuffs, fish processing, iron and steel, wood and wood products, transport equipment, cement, textiles (2003 est.)
Foreign trade:
Exports—$67.64 billion: copper, fruit, fish products, paper and pulp, chemicals, wine
Imports—$44 billion: petroleum and petroleum products, chemicals, electrical and telecommunications equipment, industrial machinery, vehicles, natural gas
Currency exchange rate: 518.65 Chilean pesos = U.S. $1 (July 2008)

* GDP = the total value of goods and services produced in a year.
All figures are 2007 estimates unless otherwise indicated. Sources: CIA World Factbook 2008; International Monetary Fund, Bloomberg.com

Manufacturing and Tourism

Chilean manufacturing is largely based on the refining and processing of the country's mineral, agricultural, and forestry resources. Chile is a major South American producer of steel. Copper is also refined, and the nation's oil refineries use both domestic and imported petroleum. Other important manufactured items include food products, cement, pulp and paper products, textiles (cotton, wool, and synthetics), tobacco products, glass, chemicals, refined sugar, and electronic equipment. The assembly of automobiles is also important. The bulk of the country's manufacturing industry is located near Santiago and Valparaíso.

By 1997 the tourism sector had become the fifth-largest source of foreign currency. Today, tourists bring about $1 billion into the country each year. Much private investment has gone into tourist centers, such as Marbella, to enable Chile to compete with such popular South American resorts as Punta del Este in Uruguay. Tourism also enjoys the support of Chile's modern transportation network, characterized by numerous and modern seaports and airports.

Foreign Investment and Future Prospects

Chile's high domestic savings and investment rates, and its openness to international trade and investment, propelled the economy to average growth rates of 8 percent during the 1990s. Chile's Foreign Investment Law entitles foreign investors to the same treatment as Chileans. Registering a company is a simple process. Foreign companies do not require a local partner. Foreigners may hold 100 percent ownership in a company, and they are entitled to all profits on which they have paid taxes. The United States is Chile's largest foreign investor, followed by Canada, Spain, and the United Kingdom.

The modern Chilean economy proved versatile in the early years of the twenty-first century. It recovered quickly from the 2002 economic crisis in neighboring Argentina, avoiding a long-term decline in foreign investment or in the value of the Chilean peso. In 2006, Chile had the highest gross domestic product (GDP) in South America. By most measures, it has become one of South America's wealthiest countries and a regional leader in economic freedom.

However, a significant income gap between the rich and the poor poses certain problems for Chile. Although poverty and unemployment rates have consistently fallen, the poorest in the country have not benefited from economic growth as much as the middle and upper classes have. In 2007, an estimated 18 percent of Chileans lived below the poverty line, a dramatic drop from nearly half the population in 1987. Still, the Chilean government acknowledges the need to aid the country's underprivileged.

Woven goods are sold at this market stall in Parinacota.

(Opposite) Local boys pose for a photo in Puerto Montt. (Right) The old Spanish church at Parinacota dates to 1610.

4 Chile's People and Culture

COMPARED WITH OTHER South American countries, Chile is not very racially diverse. Combined, *mestizos* (persons of mixed European and Native American ancestry) and a small number of whites make up slightly more than 95 percent of the population, with Indians accounting for a little less than 5 percent. This high percentage of mestizos among Chile's people has made race a minor issue. But tensions over class and social standing, a left-over from colonial times, continue to be a source of tension.

Chile is home to a number of immigrant groups, including minority populations from almost every European country. In the mid-19th century, a small but steady stream of Irish and English immigrants arrived in Chile. German immigration began in 1848 and lasted for 90 years. Other significant

A native woman and her child wear straw hats to protect themselves from the sun. The majority of Chile's population are mestizo, of mixed white and native heritage; just under 5 percent are Amerindian.

immigrant groups include Italians, Croatians, French, Basques, and Palestinians.

Among the 4.6 percent of Chile's population that claims pure Native American ancestry, the most significant groups are the Aymara, in the north, and the Mapuche, who continue to inhabit the forested areas of the Lake District.

Spanish is Chile's official language, though a handful of native languages are still spoken. These include Aymara in northern Chile, and Mapuche in the south. The most unusual minority language is preserved by the 2,000 or so speakers of Rapa Nui, the Polynesian language of most of Easter Island's population.

About 70 percent of Chileans are Roman Catholic. Church and state were officially separated in 1925, but reminders of Roman Catholicism's importance, past and present, can be seen almost everywhere, from grand colonial churches to roadside shrines containing beautiful displays of folk art. About 16 percent of Chileans practice Protestantism, with evangelical sects in particular making significant inroads in recent years. The Jewish faith and traditional Native American religions account for a negligible proportion of Chile's believers.

Chilean Culture

Historically, Europe has exerted a major influence on Chilean culture, including the country's art, architecture, music, museums, and fashion. In turn, Chile's culture—especially its art, literature, and music—have won international recognition. Chilean poets Gabriela Mistral and Pablo Neruda were awarded Nobel Prizes in literature, and the highly regarded contemporary novelist Isabel Allende is the daughter of Chile's former president. Until Augusto Pinochet's military coup of 1973, Chile's cinema was among the most experimental in Latin America. Folk music has been an especially important outlet for the country's poor and oppressed. It became popular in Spain, Italy, and Portugal during Pinochet's reign.

Chile's culture, in fact, is made up of two major competing elements: the sophisticated, cosmopolitan culture of the city

Pablo Neruda (born Ricardo Neftalí Reyes in 1904; died 1973) is considered one of the greatest Latin American poets. His most famous works include *Veinte poemas de amor y una canción desesperada* (Twenty Love Poems and a Song of Despair, 1924) and *Canto general* (1943), an epic poem about South America. He received the Nobel Prize in literature in 1971.

dwellers, and the popular culture of the peasants, which is mainly Spanish but contains traces of Indian heritage. Indian influence is strongest in Chilean music and dance.

Chile's most important museums are concentrated in the large cities of the central region. These include the National Museum of Fine Arts, the National Historical Museum, and the National Museum of Natural History, all located in Santiago, along with the Natural History Museum in Valparaíso. The Salvador Allende Museum of Solidarity, which features contemporary works by artists from around the world, opened in Santiago in 1999. The country's largest library is the National Library in Santiago, with about 3.5 million volumes.

Chilean Cuisine

Chile's cuisine reflects the country's combination of mountains, plateaus and plains, and sea. It features seafood, beef, fresh fruit, and vegetables.

A plate of *curanto*, a seafood, meat, and potato stew, in a Chilean restaurant.

Quick Facts: The People of Chile

Population: 16,454,143

Ethnic groups: white and white-Amerindian, 95.4%; Mapuche, 4%; other indigenous groups, 0.6% (2002 est.)

Age structure:
0–14 years: 23.6%
15–64 years: 67.6%
65 years and over: 8.8%

Population growth rate: 0.905%

Birth rate: 14.82 births/1,000 population

Death rate: 5.77 deaths/1,000 population

Infant mortality rate: 7.9 deaths/1,000 live births

Life expectancy at birth:
total population: 77.15 years
male: 73.88 years
female: 80.59 years

Total fertility rate: 1.95 children born/woman

Religions: Roman Catholic 70%, Evangelical 15.1%, Jehovah's Witness 1.1%, other Christian 1%, other 4.6%, none 8.3% (2002 est.)

Languages: Spanish (official); Mapuche, Aymara, and other Amerindian languages are spoken by relatively small numbers

Literacy rate: (age 15 and over who can read and write): 95.7% (2002 est.)

All figures are 2008 estimates unless otherwise indicated. Sources: CIA World Factbook 2008.

Empanadas are large turnover snacks with a variety of fillings. *Humitas* are corn tamales; a variety of potato and flour-based breads are also eaten.

Chile's most typical meal is *lomo a lo pobre*—an enormous slab of beef topped with two fried eggs and buried in potato chips. The *parillada* is a mixed grill including such delicacies as intestines, udders, and blood sausages. *Curanto*, one of the nation's finest dishes, is an all-encompassing, hearty stew of fish, shellfish, chicken, pork, lamb, beef, and potato.

Chilean wines are among South America's best. A *pisco* sour is a popular drink for adult parties. It's a grape brandy made from Chilean grapes, served with lemon juice, egg white, and powdered sugar.

(Opposite) Vacationers crowd the beach at Valparaíso. Chile's fifth-largest city is a popular tourist resort, as well as the country's major port. (Right) Rooftops in Punta Arenas. Its location on the Strait of Magellan makes Punta Arenas the southern-most city on earth.

5 Old Cities with Fresh Outlooks

JULY 2008 ESTIMATES put the population of Chile at 16,454,143, and about 88 percent of these people live in urban centers, most in the Central Valley. In fact, about 4 in 10 Chileans reside in or around the capital city, Santiago. By contrast, communities both in the south and in the northern desert tend to be more isolated; sometimes vast, almost completely unpopulated stretches lie between a town or village and its nearest neighbor.

Here are descriptions of some of the most interesting cities in Chile:

Santiago

Founded in 1541 by the Spanish conquistador Pedro de Valdivia, Santiago was burned by the Mapuche Indians six months later. Although it was immediately rebuilt on the same layout, the Spaniards deserted the

With a metropolitan-area population of more than 6 million, Santiago is the largest city in Chile.

settlement nine years later. Their interests shifted north, where they founded a number of cities. But a great Mapuche uprising in 1599 forced the Spaniards to vacate the entire area south of the Bío-Bío River. Many of the displaced settlers returned to Santiago, which became the capital of the country.

The city grew along the classic Spanish colonial model. Streets in a gridlike pattern formed small squares around a central main square. This system was maintained until the end of the 19th century. But even today in some of the older areas, it's possible to see evidence of Santiago's 16th-century past.

The heart of Santiago is the recently remodeled Plaza de Armas. On its western side is the city's Roman Catholic cathedral (completed in 1789), the fourth erected on the same site. The previous three were destroyed by fire or earthquake. A door on its south side leads to the Museo de la Catedral, which

contains religious art and historical documents. Next to it is the Palacio Arzobispal, the archbishop's palace.

On the northern side are the buildings housing the Central Post Office and the City Hall, both national monuments from colonial days. The Palacio de la Real Audiencia stands between them, housing the Museo Histórico Nacional. On the eastern and southern sides of the square there are arcades with shops. Just off the Plaza de Armas, on Calle Merced, is the Casa Colorada, Santiago's best-preserved colonial house, erected in 1769. Now it houses the Museo de Santiago, which chronicles the history of the city.

Santiago is Chile's administrative, cultural, economic, political, and industrial center. Politically, it is still the most influential city in Chile despite the fact that Congress has been moved to Valparaíso. Forty percent of the country's gross domestic product originates here. And Santiago's metropolitan area is home to more than 6 million, about 40 percent of the nation's total population.

Concepción

About 320 miles (515 km) south of Santiago, at the mouth of the Bío-Bío River, lies Concepción. From 1565 until 1573, it was the political and military capital of the Kingdom of Chile, when Chile was part of the Viceroyalty of Peru under the Spanish crown. The original site of Concepción was farther north, but a tremendous earthquake and tidal wave destroyed the town in 1751. In 1764 Concepción was moved to its present location.

Musicians perform in a Catholic festival in Achao. About 70 percent of the population of Chile is Roman Catholic.

According to Chile's 2002 census, Concepción was the 10th-largest city in the country. It is a thriving center of industrial, commercial, and cultural life. A tour of the city should start at Independence Square, with its leafy trees and its central fountain, erected in 1865 of pink stone topped with a statue of the Roman goddess Ceres, the patron of agriculture. Nearby is El Mercado (the Market), built following the earthquake of 1931, with its storefronts featuring florists, handicrafts, and inexpensive restaurants.

Another site of special interest to visitors is the Palacio de los Tribunales, on the beautiful Avenida Pedro Aguirre Cerda. This courthouse features bold columns of marble. Nearby is the Pinacoteca, or Art Museum of Concepción, housing the most extensive collection of works by Chilean painters. Two blocks away is the campus of the University of Concepción, whose buildings are grouped around a central *quadrangle* in the center of which is the Campanile, a distinctive clock tower that also serves as the emblem of the university.

Temuco

Temuco, a city on the Cautín River, is the gateway to Chile's Lake District—one of the country's most popular tourist areas. The Lake District has outstanding national parks, renowned lake resorts, volcanoes, ski resorts, and Mapuche settlements where indigenous traditions are still kept alive.

Temuco was founded in 1881 after the Mapuche Indians finally signed a peace treaty with the Chilean government. Initially it was a fort, like several other towns in the area, such as Curacautín, Victoria, Lonquimay, Villarrica, and Pucón. Because of its position near the edge of Mapuche land, Temuco was for a number of years referred to as "the Frontier Capital."

Two early developments contributed to Temuco's rapid growth: the railway and the arrival of European immigrants. Today, Temuco is a prosperous, modern city of more than 240,000, at the center of local tourism and farming. It is also a major market for Mapuche art and handicrafts.

Antofagasta

Perched on a long, narrow strip of land at the foot of the Coastal Range, Antofagasta is the largest city in Chile's far north, a major shipping port for the copper, nitrate, and other minerals mined in the region. It has also become a popular vacation destination, boasting a balmy climate and miles of beaches. One of the coastline's most dramatic vistas is provided by La Portada, a huge rock arch that stands offshore about 10 miles (16 km) north of Antofagasta.

The city itself has its share of attractions, including well-tended parks and charming architecture. The mining boom of the late 19th century brought many foreigners to Antofagasta, and the city retains a European feel. Its Barrio Histórico features many historic Victorian buildings, and standing in the Plaza Colón is an exact replica of Big Ben, London's famous clock tower.

Inland of Antofagasta, the desert is dotted with ghost mining towns, easily accessible from the Pan-American Highway. In the Altiplano flatlands of this region is the fabulous Salar de Atacama, with quaint pre-Columbian villages and Inca ruins scattered throughout the *sierra*.

Antofagasta's rise is attributable partly to natural resources and partly to natural disasters. In the early 1700s, the Spaniards set up a customs outpost and a port at Cobija, 81 miles (130 km) north of the site of present-day Antofagasta. After Bolivia won its independence from Spain, Cobija became the nation's only seaport. Antofagasta, founded around 1870 on Bolivian territory, remained a tiny town for several years until a Chilean prospector named José Díaz Gana discovered the very rich Caracoles silver vein nearby. This, combined with the area's growing nitrate mining and export trade, swelled the town's population to about 8,000—most of whom were Chilean nationals—by 1877. That year an earthquake and tidal wave leveled Cobija, making Antofagasta potentially important as an alternative port for Bolivia. In February 1879, however, Chilean troops stormed Antofagasta, triggering the War of the Pacific. At the conclusion of the conflict, Bolivia was forced to cede its entire coastline, including Antofagasta, to victorious Chile.

A New Year's Eve celebration on the beach at Renaca.

A Calendar of Chilean Festivals

As in other Latin American countries, many Chilean holidays and festivals have a basis in Roman Catholicism, the nation's principal religion. Towns and villages host festivals on the feast days of their patron saints. Children also celebrate the feast day of the saint for whom they were named, almost like a second birthday.

January

Chileans, like people in other countries, celebrate **New Year's** with fireworks at midnight and festive parties with family and friends.

February

On February 2, the north-central town of Copiapó honors the **Virgen de la Candelaria** (Virgin of Candlemas), patron saint of miners. The celebrations include dancing and folklore, but the highlight is a religious procession through the streets during which a select group of men carries a statue of the Virgin. The honor of carrying the statue in the procession is passed down from father to son.

Also in February, the city of Viña del Mar holds the **Festival de la Canción**, the largest musical contest in Latin America. Contestants from all over the world compete for the "Seagull Trophy."

March

Carnaval (Carnival), a festival preceding the solemn Catholic season of Lent, may be held in March or April, depending on when Easter falls in a given year. In Chile, Carnaval is celebrated only in the north, and Aymara Indian influences are especially noticeable in the festivities.

April

In predominantly Roman Catholic Chile, **Semana Santa** (Holy Week), which leads up to **Easter**, is an important time of year. (It may fall in March or April.) Catholics attend Mass and spend time with family.

In villages throughout central Chile, the Sunday after Easter is celebrated as the festival of **Domingo de Cuasimodo**. People decorate their houses, don colorful costumes, and parade through the village on horseback, holding images of Christ. Accompanied by cowboys, priests ride in carriages and give Communion to the elderly and sick.

May

May 1 is **Día de los Trabajadores**, a holiday honoring workers.

Glorias Navales (Navy Day) is held on May 21, the anniversary of the 1879 naval battle of Iquique. Though the outgunned Chileans lost that battle in the War of the Pacific, they demonstrated their valor by refusing to surrender to the Peruvians. Today parades, speeches, and yacht races mark the holiday.

June

The **Feast of Saints Peter and Paul**, on June 29, honors two important figures in the early history of the Roman Catholic Church, who are also

A Calendar of Chilean Festivals

among the most popular saints throughout Latin America. Chile's fishermen in particular honor St. Peter, the patron saint of fishermen, by decorating their boats and by carrying his image through the streets of their villages in hopes of enjoying bountiful catches during the coming year.

July

In mid-July the tiny village of La Tirana, on the edge of the Atacama Desert near Iquique, hosts a festival in honor of **La Virgen del Carmen**, Chile's patron saint. Tens of thousands of the faithful travel to the area, where local people are said to have seen an apparition of the Virgin. But the two-day festival is more than simply a religious pilgrimage. It includes traditional Indian music and nonstop dancing by troupes of colorfully costumed performers from around the country.

August

On August 15, Chilean Catholics celebrate the **Assumption of the Virgin Mary**. This holy day commemorates the taking up into heaven of Jesus' mother.

September

September 18 marks Chile's most important civic holiday, **Independence Day**, which is followed by **Army Day** on the 19th. The two-day festivities feature a large military parade in Santiago and smaller parades all around the country. A rodeo accompanies the festivities in many areas.

October

Many Latin Americans have mixed emotions about **Columbus Day** (October 12) because the arrival of Europeans in the New World in 1492 marked the beginning of the destruction of many native cultures. But Chile continues to observe the traditional holiday, which other countries in South and Central America celebrate as Día de la Raza—emphasizing the many races and cultures that make up Latin America.

November

In Chile, Roman Catholicism's **All Saints' Day**, November 1, is celebrated as a national holiday.

Chilean families mark **All Souls' Day** (November 2) by visiting cemeteries and remembering deceased relatives through storytelling and picnicking.

December

December 8 marks the **Immaculate Conception**. In Chile the Catholic holy day, which commemorates the freedom from original sin of Jesus' mother, Mary, is a public holiday.

Christmas occurs in the Southern Hemisphere's summer, and many Chileans celebrate with family barbecues or outings to the beach. Most attend Mass on Christmas Eve.

Chilean customs for **New Year's Eve** include eating a spoonful of lentils for good luck and putting money in one's pockets in hopes of enjoying prosperity during the coming year.

Recipes

Tomatican (**Chilean stew**)

(Serves 4)
2 cups chopped onion
1 fresh chile, minced (or quartered)
1 tsp cayenne pepper
2 tbsp olive oil
2 tsp ground cumin
2 cups frozen lima beans
1 or 2 cans whole tomatoes (28 oz. total)
2 cups frozen cut corn
1/4 cup chopped fresh cilantro
Grated cheddar or Monterey Jack cheese
1 avocado, peeled, then cubed or sliced

Directions:
1. Drain the tomatoes, reserving the juice.
2. In a heavy soup pot or saucepan, sauté the onions and chile or cayenne in the olive oil for about 5 minutes, until the onions begin to soften.
3. Add the cumin and lima beans and sauté, stirring, for a couple of minutes.
4. Add the juice from the tomatoes, cover, and simmer for 5 minutes.
5. Chop the whole tomatoes right in the can. Stir the chopped tomatoes and corn into the pan. Cover and simmer until the vegetables are tender.
6. Stir in cilantro and add salt and black pepper to taste.
7. Serve over rice, polenta, or quinoa, or with warm tortillas or cornbread.

Avocado and Zucchini Soup

(Serves 6)
4 cups vegetable broth
1 lb zucchini, finely sliced
2 avocados, peeled
1/2 cup plain yogurt
3 tbsp lemon juice
2 tsp Worcestershire or soy sauce
3/4 tsp ground coriander
Pinch of salt
1/2 tsp sugar
Dash of Tabasco
1 cup diced tomatoes, seeded

Directions:
1. In a saucepan heat the vegetable broth.
2. Add zucchini and simmer until very soft, about 10 minutes.
3. Remove zucchini from pan with slotted spoon and reserve the cooking liquid.
4. In a blender or food processor, puree zucchini with the avocados.
5. Put the puree in the saucepan and stir in the yogurt, lemon juice, Worcestershire or soy sauce, coriander, salt, sugar, and Tabasco. Heat thoroughly but do not boil.
6. Spoon into soup bowls and garnish on top with the tomatoes.

Grape Zucchini Quick Bread

(Makes 1 loaf, or about 10 servings)
1 cup green seedless grapes
1 cup all-purpose flour
1 cup wheat germ
1 tsp baking powder
1 tsp baking soda
1 cup sunflower seeds
1 egg
1 cup salad oil
1 cup white sugar
1 cup packed brown sugar
1 tsp almond or vanilla extract
1 cup shredded zucchini
Sesame seeds

Directions:
1. Preheat oven to 350°F.
2. Rinse and drain grapes thoroughly.
3. In a bowl, blend flour, wheat germ, baking powder, soda, salt, and sunflower seeds.
4. In another bowl, beat together egg, oil, sugars, and almond or vanilla extract.
5. Add zucchini and grapes to egg mixture; then gently pour into flour mixture and stir.
6. Pour batter into an oiled and flour-dusted 5" x 9" loaf pan. Sprinkle top of loaf with sesame seed.
7. Bake for 1 hour or until a toothpick inserted into center of loaf comes out clean. Cool 10 minutes and remove from pan to a wire rack. Slice and serve.

Chilean Sweet-Corn Wraps

(Serves 5–6)
8 large Chinese cabbage leaves
1 can of sweet corn (15 oz.), drained
4 tbsp milk
2 eggs, beaten
2 tbsp finely chopped fresh herbs (marjoram, basil, coriander, etc.)
Pepper to taste
Toothpicks

Directions:
1. Steam the Chinese cabbage leaves for a minute or two until supple but not too soft.
2. In a blender, turn all the rest of the ingredients together to a paste.
3. Divide the mixture into eight and put spoonfuls into the center of each cabbage leaf. Wrap up like an egg roll, with the ends folded in, and secure with a wooden toothpick.
4. Steam over hot water for 20–25 minutes until the filling is set. (Don't put the wraps in water; put them in a basket above steaming water.)
5. Serve with rice or noodles.

Glossary

affluence—an abundance of property or wealth.

archipelago—a group of islands.

cascades—small, steep falls in a stream or river.

climatological—having to do with climate.

conquistador—a leader in the Spanish conquest of Central and South America during the 16th century.

cordillera—a chain of mountains.

depose—to remove a leader from a throne or high public office.

dissidents—citizens who disagree with their government; protesters.

domestic—local; created inside a country.

fjord—a narrow inlet of sea between cliffs or mountains.

headland—a point of high land jutting out into a body of water.

indigenous—native or original to a region.

inflation—the increasing cost of goods and services in an economy over a period of time.

junta—a group of persons controlling a government after a takeover.

oligarchy—a government in which a small group exercises control, often for selfish purposes; also, a group exercising such control.

Glossary

plebiscite—a vote by an entire country to express an opinion for or against a proposal.

quadrangle—a four-sided enclosure surrounded by buildings.

sierra—a range of mountains with irregular peaks.

Socialist—a person who supports collective or governmental ownership of the means of production and distribution of goods.

temperate—having a mild climate.

topographic—having to do with natural or man-made surface features of a place or region.

Project and Report Ideas

Reports

Write a one-page, three-paragraph report answering any of the following questions. Begin with a paragraph of introduction, then a paragraph developing a main idea, followed by a conclusion that summarizes your topic:

- Why is the Atacama Desert one of the driest places on earth?
- How were the first Spanish explorers in Chile "greeted" by the Indians?
- Why are the Andes Mountains said to be still growing?
- How is copper mined and processed?
- Why is the Strait of Magellan so treacherous?
- What is a Mediterranean climate, and where does it occur in the world?
- What happened in 2002 in Argentina that has negatively affected the economy of Chile and other South American nations?
- How is inflation a serious economic problem for any nation?

Write a one-page, three-paragraph biography of any one of the following people:

Diego de Almagro	Bernardo O'Higgins
José de San Martín	Salvador Allende
Isabel Allende	Augusto Pinochet
Gabriela Mistral	Pablo Neruda

Assemble a list of the best websites for finding out about Chile. Devise a rating system. Include a one- or two-sentence summary about the site. Combine these sites in a comprehensive guide to Chile on the Internet for other classes to use.

Maps

- Make a map enlarging the tip of South America. Show how ships of the world cross from the Atlantic to the Pacific Oceans.
- Make a climatological map showing the three zones of Chile—arid, Mediterranean, and temperate marine.

Project and Report Ideas

Presentations

Pretend that you were an exchange student in Chile last year. Share your scrapbook with the class. Do the following:

- Present a color picture of the Chilean flag.
- Find an example of Chilean currency (major airport currency exchanges and some banks carry it). Find out what the exchange rate is.
- Prepare a map, and highlight the city in which you "lived." Pronounce the Spanish name correctly.
- Show some of the famous and/or vacation places on the map that you visited with "family." Why are they famous? Supply pictures.
- Play some music from the country.
- Read aloud several poems by Pablo Neruda. Rehearse them so that you are able to glance up from the text. Be prepared to explain why the poet chose certain words to create images or feelings.

All-Class Video

For a glimpse into what it's like being a poet, watch the award-winning Italian film *Il Postino* (The Postman). A humble postman delivers mail to Pablo Neruda, who is living in exile from his native Chile. The two become friends, and Neruda's encouragement leads the postman to try writing poetry, with remarkable results.

Chronology

15th century	Incas moving south encounter the Mapuche, one of the three Araucanian peoples in the land of present-day Chile, who halt their advance down the Central Valley.
1535	Setting out from Peru, Diego de Almagro leads first Spanish expedition to explore and conquer the lands of present-day Chile; two-year journey, filled with hardships, is largely unsuccessful.
1540	Pedro de Valdivia resumes Spanish efforts to conquer Chile.
1541	Santiago is founded.
1553	After slowly pushing the Araucanians south past the Bío-Bío River, founding various settlements, and serving as Chile's first colonial governor, Valdivia is killed in fighting with the Indians.
Late 1500s	Araucanian resistance forces the Spanish north of the Bío-Bío River, a line of separation that will remain until the 1800s.
17th/18th centuries	Large agricultural estates develop in Chile. They are owned by a few criollo families and worked by the large class of landless and impoverished mestizos.
1808	Napoleon Bonaparte, France's emperor, deposes the Spanish king, Ferdinand VII, and places his brother on the throne.
1810	Professing their loyalty to Ferdinand VII, a group of Chileans seizes the government of their colony on September 18; soon José Miguel Carrera and Bernardo O'Higgins emerge as rivals in the fight for full independence from Spain.
1814	Ferdinand is restored to the Spanish throne; in Chile, at the Battle of Rancagua, royalist troops decisively defeat O'Higgins, who flees to Argentina.
1817	O'Higgins, joining forces with José de San Martín, crosses the Andes into Chile and defeats the royalists at the Battle of Chacabuco; he is made supreme director of Chile.
1818	Under the leadership of O'Higgins, Chileans declare their independence from Spain on February 12.
1823	O'Higgins is ousted and forced into exile in Peru.

1881	Chilean government signs a treaty with Argentina confirming Chilean sovereignty over the Strait of Magellan, the primary sea-lane connecting the Atlantic and Pacific Oceans.
1879–83	Chile fights Peru and Bolivia in the War of the Pacific; by winning that war, Chile expands its territory northward by almost one-third.
Late 1800s	European immigrants arrive in large numbers in Chile.
1970	By a slim margin, voters elect Dr. Salvador Allende, a Socialist intellectual who believes that workers should control the production of goods and services.
1973	The military, led by General Augusto Pinochet, storms the presidential palace on September 11. Allende dies during the fighting. Pinochet becomes military dictator.
1980	A new constitution is approved by a plebiscite and General Pinochet becomes President of the Republic for an eight-year term.
1988	In another plebiscite, Chileans vote for elections to choose a new president and the majority of members of a two-chamber congress. Pinochet is turned out.
1989	Voters elect Christian Democrat Patricio Aylwin, the candidate of a coalition of 17 political parties, to the presidency in December.
2000	Pinochet is arrested in London on a warrant by a Spanish judge investigating violations of human rights in Chile, but he is later declared too ill to stand trial; in Chile, Ricardo Lagos Escobar wins a narrow victory in presidential elections.
2001	An appeals court in Chile rules Augusto Pinochet, under house arrest since December 2000, mentally unfit to be tried for killings committed under his regime.
2002	Santiago hosts the United Nations Convention on Trade in Endangered Species.
2004	President Lagos approves a law permitting Chileans to divorce; Chile signs a trade agreement with the United States.
2006	Former Minister of Defense Michelle Bachelet Jeria is elected president; Augusto Pinochet dies of heart failure.
2008	Chatién volcano erupts for the first time in 9,400 years; 5,000 people are forced to evacuate.

Further Reading/Internet Resources

Beech, Charlotte, et al. *Chile and Easter Island.* Oakland, Calif.: Lonely Planet, 2007.

Chester, Sharon. *A Wildlife Guide to Chile.* Princeton, N.J.: Princeton University Press, 2008.

Dipiazza, Francesca Davis. *Chile in Pictures.* Minneapolis: Lerner Publications, 2007.

Perrone, Caterina. *Chile: A Quick Guide to Customs and Etiquette.* London: Kuperard, 2007.

Rector, John L. *The History of Chile.* London: Palgrave Macmillan, 2005.

Travel Information

http://www.lonelyplanet.com/worldguide/chile-and-easter-island/
http://www.worldtravelguide.net/country/57/country_guide/South-America/Chile.html
http://www.travelnotes.org/LatinAmerica/chile.htm

History and Geography

http://www.hartford-hwp.com/archives/42a/index-d.html
http://www.geographia.com/chile/chilehistory.htm
http://www.gorp.com/gorp/location/latamer/chile/chil_pks.htm

Economic and Political Information

http://www.state.gov/r/pa/ei/bgn/1981.htm
https://www.cia.gov/library/publications/the-world-factbook/geos/ci.html

For More Information

U.S. Department of Commerce
Trade Information Center
International Trade Administration
14th and Constitution Ave., NW
Washington, DC 20230
Websites: http://www.export.gov and http://www.buyusa.gov/chile

Embassy of the Republic of Chile
1732 Massachusetts Ave., NW
Washington, DC 20036
(202) 785-1746
E-mail: embassy@embassyofchile.org

Chilean Consulate General
Sixth Floor, Suite 601
866 United Nations Plaza
New York, NY 10017
(212) 355 0612
E-mail: secretaria@chileny.com
Website: http://www.chileny.com

American Chamber of Commerce in Chile
Vespucio Sur 80, Piso 9
82 Correo 34 Santiago
Chile
562-290-9700
Website: http://www.amchamchile.cl

Index

Aconcagua, 12
Aconcagua River, 13, 15
Allende, Isabel, 39
Allende, Salvador, 24, 25, 30
Almagro, Diego de, 20
Andes Mountains, 9, 12, 13, 14, 17, 19, 22
Antarctic Circle, 9
Antofagasta, 16, 48–49
Argentina, 11, 13, 22, 23, 30, 34
Asia-Pacific Economic Cooperation (APEC), 30
Atacama Desert, 9, 13, 17, 19
Aylwin, Patricio, 26
Aymara, 38

Bachelet, Michelle, 27
Beagle Channel, 12
Bío-Bío River, 13, 15, 20, 44, 46
Bolivia, 11, 23, 49
Bonaparte, Joseph, 22
Bonaparte, Napoleon, 22
Brazil, 29, 30

Cape Horn, 11, 14
Carrera, José Miguel, 22
Cerro Aconcagua. *See* Aconcagua
Chacabuco, battle of, 22

Chile
  culture of, 39–41
  economy of, 24–25, 29–35
  foreign investment in, 34–35
  geography of, 9–17
  history of, 19–27
  indigenous people of, 14, 19–21, 37, 38, 40
  museums in, 40
  people of, 37–38
  plants and animals of, 17
  possessions of, 11–12
Chiloé Island, 11
Chonos Archipelago, 11
Cobija, 49
Concepción, 46–47
copper, 29–30
Curacautín, 47
Cuzco, 19

Drake Passage, 12

Easter Island, 12, 38
Elqui River, 15
Escobar, Ricardo Lagos, 27
European Union, 29

Ferdinand VII, king of Spain, 22
Frei-Montalva, Eduardo, 23

Gana, José Díaz, 49
Imperial River, 15
Incas, 19, 20

Juan Fernández Islands, 12

Lake District, 9, 14, 38, 47
Llanquihue, Lake, 14
Loa River, 15
Lonquimay, 47

Maipo River, 15
Mapuche, 19, 23, 38, 43, 44, 47, 48
Marbella, 34
Maule River, 15, 19
Mistral, Gabriela, 39

Neruda, Pablo, 39
North American Free Trade Agreement (NAFTA), 30

O'Higgins, Bernardo, 22
Ojos del Salado, 12

Pacific Ocean, 11, 12, 14, 23
Paraguay, 30
Patagonia, 14, 31
Peru, 11, 19, 20, 23, 46
Pinochet, Augusto, 25, 26, 30, 39

Index/Picture Credits

Pizarro, Francisco, 20
Puerto Montt, 15
Punta Arenas, 17
Punta del Este, 34

Rancagua, battle of, 22
Rapa Nui, 38
Ruiz-Tagle, Eduardo Frei, 26

Sala y Gómez, 12
San Martín, José de, 22
Santiago, 15, 16, 20, 22, 34,
    43–46

Southern Cone Common
    Market (MERCOSUR), 30
Strait of Magellan, 12, 14, 17,
    23

Temuco, 47
Tierra del Fuego, 11–12, 31
Tropic of Capricorn, 9

United States, 29
Uruguay, 30, 34

Valdivia, Pedro de, 20, 43

Valparaíso, 34
Victoria, 47
Villarrica, 47

War of the Pacific, 23, 49
Wellington Island, 11
World War I, 29

Contributors

Senior Consulting Editor **James D. Henderson** is professor of international studies at Coastal Carolina University. He is the author of *Conservative Thought in Twentieth Century Latin America: The Ideals of Laureano Gómez* (1988; Spanish edition *Las ideas de Laureano Gómez* published in 1985); *When Colombia Bled: A History of the Violence in Tolima* (1985; Spanish edition *Cuando Colombia se desangró, una historia de la Violencia en metrópoli y provincia*, 1984); and coauthor of *A Reference Guide to Latin American History* (2000) and *Ten Notable Women of Latin America* (1978).

Mr. Henderson earned a bachelor's degree in history from Centenary College of Louisiana, and a master's degree in history from the University of Arizona. He then spent three years in the Peace Corps, serving in Colombia, before earning his doctorate in Latin American history in 1972 at Texas Christian University.

Charles J. Shields is the author of 20 books for young people. He has degrees in English and history from the University of Illinois, Urbana-Champaign. Before turning to writing full time, he was chairman of the English and guidance departments at Homewood-Flossmoor High School in Flossmoor, Illinois. He lives in Homewood, a suburb of Chicago, with his wife, Guadalupe, a former elementary school principal and now an educational consultant to the Chicago Public Schools.